Illustrated
Stories *from the* Bible

Volume 1

AUTHORS
George and Marilyn Durrant
Former Professor of Ancient Scriptures

Educational Doctorate

ARTIST AND ART DIRECTOR
Vernon Murdock
Artist Illustrator

Bachelor of Fine Arts
Graduate Work, University of Madrid,
Spain

CORRELATORS AND DIRECTORS
Steven R. Shallenberger, *President*
Community Press, Wisdom House, Eagle
Marketing Corporation

Bachelor of Science; Accounting, Business.
SCMP, Graduate School of Business, Harvard
University.

Paul R. Cheesman
Director of Scripture in Religious Study Center
Chaplain, U.S. Navy

Doctor of Religious Education

Lael J. Woodbury
Chairman, National Committee on Royalties,
American Theatre Association

Doctorate of Theater, University of Illinois

ADVISORS
Dale T. Tingey
Director American Indian Services and
Research Center

Doctor of Philosophy, Guidance and
Counseling; Washington State University

Reverend Raymond E. Ansel
Ordained Minister

Southwestern Assemblies of God College, Texas
Berean Bible School, Missouri

Millie Foster Cheesman
Writer, Poetess

Reverend William R. Schroeder
United Church of Christ

United Theological Seminary of the Twin Cities
New Brighton, Minnesota

SECOND EDITION VOLUME 1, 1981
Fourth Printing January 1984

Lithographed in U.S.A.
by
COMMUNITY PRESS, INC.
P.O. Box 1229
Antioch, California 94509

A member of
The American Bookseller's Association
New York, New York

FOREWORD

"Train up a child in the way he should go: and when he is old, he will not depart from it." (Proverbs 22:6)

We have been in the business of developing and providing families with religious educational products for fifteen years. There have been many requests to produce a set of books about the Old and New Testaments. This set of books is the cumulation of years of preparation and work to provide parents and students of the scriptures with the finest teaching tool available on the Bible.

It is unique to any other set available in that the scriptures and stories are told by illustrations and photographs. In addition to vivid illustrations being available, a dramatized cassette tape has been produced to accompany each volume. These aids seem to make the stories come alive.

Each set of illustrations re-creates a story that has some type of moral lesson to it. At the end of each segment a few questions are provided to provoke thought in applying a gospel principle.

Dr. George Durrant, a noted teacher and author, has done a masterful job in presenting the stories in an interesting, simple, and concise manner so that they may be read and understood by young children. We also thank Marilyn, his wife, for her countless hours of research and help in preparing the *Illustrated Bible Stories*. Being the parents of eight children, the Durrants have a keen insight into the viewpoint of a young child.

We feel fortunate to have Mr. Vernon Murdock as the illustrator for the series. He has done an exceptional job in portraying the ideas and concepts of this sacred record.

We are also grateful to the many individuals who have made contributions, suggestions, and critiques.

To Bea Friel and the staff of Community Press for their excellent work in the preparation of these volumes for the final printing.

We truly hope that this set of books will be a great influence in your life and the lives of your family members.

Steven R. Shallenberger, *President*
Eagle Systems International

Dedicated to boys and girls throughout the world and to all who love the Bible.

Presented to _____

By _____

Date _____

A *non-denominational work.*

CONTENTS

When I consider thy heavens, the work of thy fingers, the moon and the stars, which thou hast ordained;

What is man, that thou art mindful of him? and the son of man, that thou visitest him?

For thou hast made him a little lower than the angels, and hast crowned him with glory and honour.

Thou madest him to have dominion over the works of thy hands; thou hast put all things under his feet:

All sheep and oxen, yea, and the beasts of the field;

The fowl of the air, and the fish of the sea, and whatsoever passeth through the paths of the seas.

O LORD our Lord, how excellent is thy name in all the earth!

Psalms 8:3-9

Smilax: a climbing plant found in the Holy Land. It has broad shiny evergreen leaves, small greenish-yellow flowers, and red berries. The young shoots are eaten like asparagus.

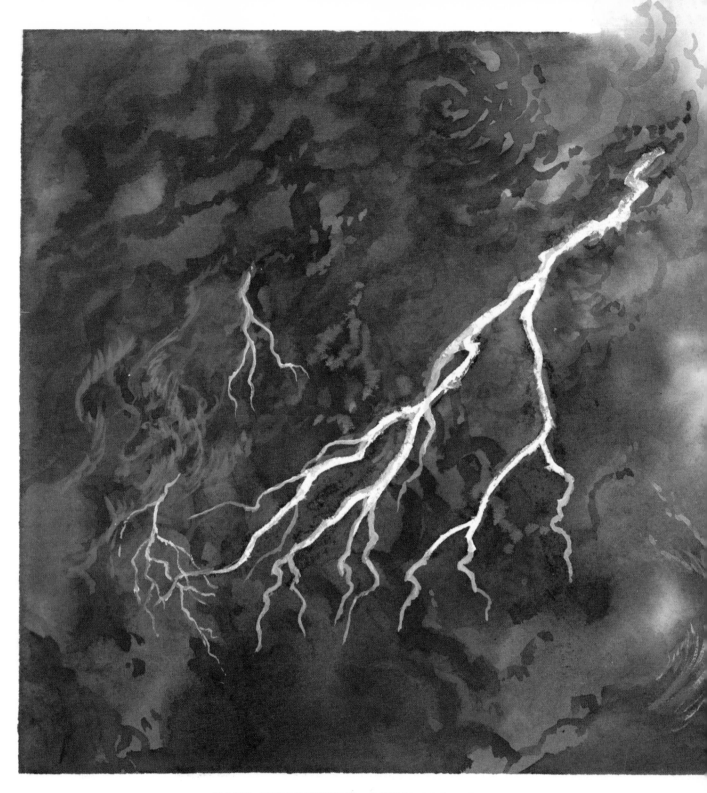

OUR BEAUTIFUL NEW HOME
Genesis Chapters 1, 2

Through the darkness of the endless space God said, "Let there be light. . . ."
At that moment a large ball-shaped mass of boiling mixture was lit up as a hillside
when lightning strikes across the sky on a stormy night. The bright glow continued
to burn on and on, lighting up the round, spinning mass which was soon to be
formed into our beautiful earth.

As the large ball cooled, a light source gave light to part of the mass while part remained in darkness. The light was called day and the darkness night. By creating light and separating it from darkness, God had begun to make the earth. The Bible states that the evening and the morning were the first day or the first period of time. With this light man would be able to see in order that he could work and play by the light of day and sleep and rest during the darkness of night.

At that time the earth was a boiling, melting ball. Because of the great volcano-like heat, moisture rose upward from this bubbling, steaming mixture. Then on the second day, by God's command, this gas and moisture became what we now call the air or atmosphere which surrounds the earth. It also became the moisture or water of the seas and oceans.

It took great knowledge and power to create light and water. But if God's power had been mighty in the first two days of the earth's creation, it was even more so on the third day. On that day the earth shook as during an earthquake and the land came up from below the water, creating waterfalls, rushing streams and rivers, and lakes. The rising land pushed the water into the lower areas and formed oceans upon the face of the new earth.

11

At the end of his work of the third day God called the dry land earth, and the places where the water had gathered he called seas. Thus were the beginnings of this wonderful planet. The earth was now formed and nearly ready for living things. God looked down from heaven and saw that all he had done in these three days was good.

Because there were no plants, grass, or trees growing on the dry land, it didn't seem as beautiful as the water with its white-capped waves, or the blue sky with its everchanging patterns of clouds. But that was no longer true when God said, "Let the earth bring forth grass. . . ." Soon a carpet of green grass covered the hillsides and the valleys. Gardens of flowers, bushes, and trees grew everywere.

Imagine how beautiful the fresh, new earth now looked. There were delicious berries, grains, fruits, and vegetables to provide food for those who would soon live on the earth. The third day had been one of much excitement. When it had ended, God looked at this earth and again was pleased, for he saw that it was good.

Anyone who has
seen the sun by day and
the moon and stars by
night might be thrilled at
what happened on the
fourth day. At that time
God's great power
reached out into space
and he created the sun to
rule and give light to the
day, adding the moon as
a lesser light to rule the
night. The stars also
appeared in the endless
sky. While the earth was
spinning as a top, circling
the sun, God had created
the variety and beauty of
the seasons—of summer,
fall, winter, and spring.

With sunlight, air, dry land, water, and plants for food, the earth was now ready for what was to happen on the fifth day. This must have been an exciting time for God since it was at this time he created the large whales and all the many other fish and sea creatures. He turned them loose to frolic and search for food in the cool, clear waters of oceans, lakes, rivers, and streams. He then made the beautiful birds, which probably sang songs of joy as he set them free to fly higher and higher.

Looking down from heaven, God saw the ocean's gentle waves drifting back and forth over the sandy beaches. Small streams were gliding across slippery rocks. Green grass and groves of trees covered the land. The fifth day had ended and on the sixth day all was ready for God's most important creation!

Anyone who loves animals would want to have been with God at this time. On this, the sixth day, God created every creature that walks upon the earth. The sun's rays shed light on the grass, which was green and wet with dew. All was in readiness to feed the beautiful, tame, but also hungry animals. Each animal was free to run about and eat the tender grasses and leaves.

Now at last the earth was ready for God's final creation. God said, "Let us make man in our image, after our likeness. . . ." God then created a body for the first man, Adam.

Adam was all alone on the earth, so God made a wife for him. Her name was Eve and she was the first woman. What an honor for man and woman to be created in the image of God! Adam and Eve were asked to care for and be masters over all other living things. They were even given the interesting job of naming each kind of animal and bird.

The creation of the earth was now complete. God, our Father in heaven, was filled with joy and love as he saw the light, the darkness, the water, the dry land, the sun, the stars, the moon, the fish, the birds, the animals, and his two happy children, Adam and Eve. During the six days God had made our earthly home. On the seventh day he rested.

Knowing the true story of the creation of the earth, it is surprising to hear some people say that the earth was not created by God. Such people believe the earth and all its beauty happened by accident. To believe this would be much like believing that one could take all the many separate parts of a clock, put them all in a paper sack, shake the sack, and expect all the parts to come together and create a clock. We know that this couldn't happen. A clock can only be made when there is a clockmaker to put it together in just the right way; and the earth could only have been made because there was a God to create it.

As we see the oceans, the mountains, the animals, the sun, the stars, or a newborn baby, it is like seeing evidences of God.

By seeing what God has created we know that he has been here. We also know that by being his offspring, God loves us and is still watching over us. Thus, as we read in all the Bible stories, we can understand that God has indeed been with his people since the time of Adam and Eve until now.

THINK ABOUT IT

1. If you could have watched just one day of the creation of the world, which day would you have chosen? Why?
2. What was God's most magnificent creation? Why do you feel that way?
3. In your prayers of gratitude what would you say to Heavenly Father to show him your thankfulness for those things which he created for you?

THE DAY THAT CHANGED EVERYTHING
Genesis Chapters 2, 3

There was no sadness in the new world and no such thing as death. But one day something happened that changed all of that and made things different for

Adam and Eve. It not only changed things for them but also for all who would live after them upon the earth. To understand what happened, one must first be aware that God had told Adam and Eve they could eat any fruit of the garden except the fruit of one certain tree. That tree was called the tree of knowledge of good and evil. They were told if they ate the fruit of that tree they would grow old and die.

Eve was alone when Satan startled her by asking, "Have you eaten of the fruit of that tree?" Eve replied that she had not. Satan spoke through a serpent or snake and said, "If you eat that fruit you won't die, but you'll be like God, knowing good from evil." Because Eve was as a child, she trusted Satan and ate some of the fruit. She went to where Adam was and he also ate. The eating of the fruit changed them. They now knew that there were right and wrong choices to make.

That evening God came to visit, but Adam and Eve felt ashamed about what they had done and they hid from him. God told them to come to him. He knew the reason they had disobeyed him was because of Satan. Adam and Eve were told that they would have to leave the garden. They were also told that children would be born to them, that Satan would tempt these children in such a way that they would sin (or in other words, disobey God), and thus these children would live in sorrow and sadness. God, being angry with Satan, warned Satan that there would come a time in the distant future when he would be crushed and all his evil work destroyed. This was when God gave his first promise that there would come a time when he would send a savior to do away with all the evil work Satan had done.

For not doing as God had told them, Adam and Eve had to leave the Garden of Eden. Their world now would be different. In the garden they would have never died. They would have remained as children and never known the difference between good and evil. Now they would live to old age and die. They would have to work and sweat to get food instead of just plucking it from trees.

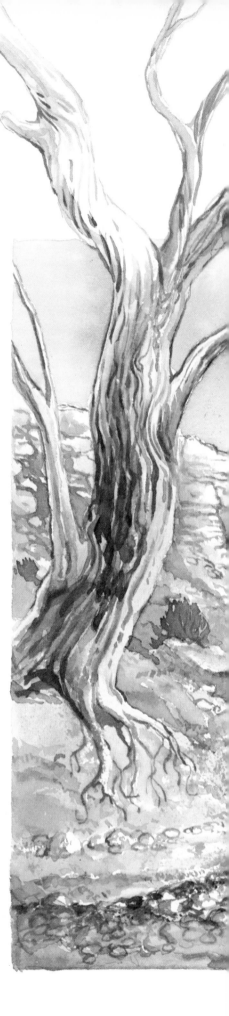

With sorrow in their hearts Adam and Eve left their garden home. An angel with a sword guarded the entrance to keep them from returning. All that kept them from giving up was the excitement of the future. Both Adam and Eve looked forward to having children and creating the first family on earth. They had faith that a savior would come to make up for what all mankind had done wrong and would crush Satan. They felt happy in their belief that someday all would live with God forever in a place like their beautiful Garden of Eden.

Just as God had promised, Adam and Eve did have children. As part of family worship they taught them to offer sacrifices to the Lord. This was done by killing an animal and placing it on an altar. The animal would then be burned and the smoke would go up toward heaven. Offering sacrifice reminded them that God himself would someday offer a great sacrifice to help them become free from sin, sorrow, and death and to once again be with God.

THINK ABOUT IT

1. Are you sad or are you glad Adam and Eve had to leave the Garden of Eden? Why?
2. Why do you think Adam and Eve looked forward to the time when Jesus Christ would be born?

THE FIRST GREAT SADNESS
Genesis Chapters 4, 5

As Cain and Abel, two of the sons of Adam and Eve, grew up, they had seen their father offer sacrifices many times. As young men they also offered sacrifices. Cain placed on his altar fruits and vegetables which he had grown. Not far away Abel offered a sacrifice of his best and fattest young animals. God was pleased with Abel's offering. Cain didn't want to offer a sacrifice to God in the first place and became very jealous when God wasn't pleased with his offering. In his heart he began to hate his brother Abel.

God knew what Cain was thinking. He told Cain to repent, or change, and then his sacrifice would be accepted. He warned Cain that if he didn't repent Satan would lead him into great sin. This seemed to make Cain even more jealous and his feelings of hatred toward Abel grew. Then one terrible day while Abel was helping Cain in the fields, Cain became so enraged that in a fit of anger he killed his brother.

Think of the tears Adam and Eve must have shed when they found the body of their son Abel. How sad they were when they learned that Cain, their other son, was a murderer who had not only killed his brother but had now run away from home. Adam and Eve remembered what God had told them about sorrow and sin. The world outside the garden could indeed be a sad place.

THINK ABOUT IT

1. Cain killed Abel, but long before he killed him he started doing something else that you and I might do if we're not careful. What was it?
2. How can we make sure we never cause the kind of sorrow Cain caused?

31

GOOD PEOPLE AND HAPPY DAYS
Genesis Chapter 5

But sadness doesn't last forever. In time a new baby was born to mother Eve. His name was Seth. Eve looked down at this smiling little infant and softly said to Adam, "God hath given me a new son to take the place of our beloved Abel." Again Adam and Eve were happy. Perhaps, they thought, this son would be the one who would crush Satan.

Seth was a good child and grew up to be a fine man. As the years passed he had sons of his own and they loved and worshipped God. Adam and Eve were proud of Seth and of his children, who were their grandchildren. Adam saw many grandchildren and great-grandchildren because he lived for nine hundred and thirty years. Methuselah, his fifth great-grandson, lived even longer than Adam. He lived 969 years and became the oldest man to ever live upon the earth.

Although Methuselah holds the record for the longest life, perhaps his father, Enoch, really deserves that record since he never died. ". . . Enoch walked with God, and God . . . took him." (Genesis 5:24)

NOAH DOES WHAT THE LORD ASKS
Genesis Chapters 5-7

Enoch had a great-grandson who grew up to be one of God's greatest prophets. Can you guess who he was? He was the mighty shipbuilder and prophet, Noah. It was hard work to build such a big ship. It's no wonder the job took 120 years! But the Lord had told Noah to build a ship (called an ark) so he did.

The evil people didn't believe Noah when he said they would be destroyed if they didn't repent and keep God's commandments. They wanted to listen to Satan, not God. Because of their great wickedness, God knew that their little children would have no chance to be good. God felt so bad about this that he cried. Why did his children love to lie and steal and be mean? God decided that all the people were so evil that it would be best to remove them from the earth and start over. God asked Noah to warn the people to change or they would be destroyed.

The people laughed, mocked, and made fun of Noah as they watched him build the ark. As the years passed, the large ship took shape and finally was completed. Now there was an important job to do that would have been impossible without God's help. For seven days Noah and his family collected a male and a female of each kind of animal and bird and put them inside the ark. Then Noah and his family entered the big three-story ark. The door clanged shut behind them and that was the last time the wicked people ever laughed at the man who had obeyed God.

A NEW BEGINNING
Genesis Chapters 7, 8

Then rain began to fall! It fell harder than ever before or since. It was like many rivers pouring down from the sky. Soon the ark tipped from side to side and finally became level as it was completely afloat. The people outside the ship were now screaming and running to higher ground, but the water level rose until all were drowned. In the days that followed, the entire earth was covered with much water. The lonely looking ship with its little group of passengers rocked to and fro upon the waves.

After forty days and forty nights Noah, his wife, and their three boys (Shem, Ham, and Japheth) and their wives were suddenly filled with hope. The sound of rain, which at first had roared and then later only pattered against the roof of the upper deck of the ark, had suddenly stopped. After the rain had stopped, the weary travelers took courage and looked out a window. As they looked they could see that the water had covered everything. All the people, the animals, and even the birds had been destroyed. Only those in the ark lived.

Slowly, very slowly, the waters began to dry up and disappear. After several months mountain peaks were seen as islands here and there. To learn if dry land was near, Noah opened a window and released a dove. If the dove returned with a twig or leaf, Noah would know that they could soon leave the huge ark that now almost seemed like home.

The dove was gone for a long time. Then, to the disappointment of the family, it returned with its beak empty. A week later the same experiment was repeated and this time a shout went up from the survivors of the great flood. In the returning dove's beak was an olive leaf. With gladness and joy, Noah and his family members and all the anxious animals once again set foot on dry ground.

As Adam had done in his day, Noah now built a stone altar and offered sacrifices to God. The world was new again. God told Noah and his family that now his children could come to a home free of the wickedness and sins that had been in the hearts of the people before the flood.

God promised Noah and his family that he would never again cause such a mighty flood to come upon the earth to destroy the people. As a sign of his promise to Noah and his family that the earth would never again be covered with water, God placed a beautiful rainbow in the sky. Man, on the other hand, should also strive to so live that such a sad thing would never again be necessary.

THINK ABOUT IT

1. What is your favorite part of the story of Noah?

A BIG BUT FOOLISH BUILDING
Genesis Chapter 11

Some 100 years had passed since the great flood. Noah's family had multiplied and grown until there were once again thousands of people upon the earth. But Satan was still around. He told the people that they should trust in their own wisdom and strength and forget God. An evil man named Nimrod, the great hunter, convinced the people that they could achieve anything by themselves and that God really wasn't needed. He persuaded them to try to build a tower that would reach all the way to heaven.

As the Lord watched his children working on such a foolish task, it saddened his heart. He may well have thought, "Why do they not believe me? I promised them there would never be another flood, yet they try to build a tower that they think would give them safety if another flood did come."

God had hoped that, as Noah's family grew, the people would go to all parts of the world. However, because of the building of the gigantic tower, all of the people were staying to help with the work. Seeing the people use all their energy on such a useless project, God put an end to the foolishness by confusing their language.

You can imagine the confusion that occurred when one worker said something such as, "Hand me a building block," and another man working nearby answered in another language, saying something such as, "Tat der spling," which could have meant, "I can't understand you."

Thus God changed the one language of the people into many languages. All of a sudden the workers couldn't understand each other. The work slowed down and nearly stopped. All the crews became disorganized, confused, and soon were very discouraged. They decided in their own minds it was no use trying to continue to build the tower. Many of them packed their possessions and went to other parts of the world, just as God had hoped they would. God surely tries every way possible to help his children avoid making mistakes and doing foolish things.

THINK ABOUT IT

1. The Tower of Babel was a foolish project. What are some of the things people do today that are as foolish as trying to build a tower to heaven?

GOD CALLS ANOTHER PROPHET
Genesis Chapters 11, 12

From the Tower of Babel the people went in all directions—building up and living in many new cities.

At this time, which was about 300 years after the flood, Satan had again turned many people against God. The people were nearly as wicked as the ones who had laughed at Noah. Many of them had learned to make beautiful things out of metal, especially gold. They made golden statues and knelt and prayed to them instead of praying to God.

Noah, who was still alive but very old, told the people in his city about the flood, the ark, and the rainbow.

However, since those things had happened so long ago, the people laughed at him. They loved their golden gods and other possessions more than they loved the God of Noah.

Even so, at this time there were still some people who were good. These good people needed a leader—someone to whom God could speak and who could then tell them what God wanted them to do. They also needed someone to tell the wicked people to change their ways and become righteous. In a city called Ur, God found such a man by the name of Abram. God later changed this man's name to Abraham and chose him to be his prophet. (A prophet is a person who receives messages from God for his children on the earth.)

And God spoke to his prophet Abraham and said, "Get thee out of thy country, . . . unto a land that I will shew thee: And I will make of thee a great nation, and I will bless thee, and make thy name great; and thou shalt be a blessing."

GOD'S GREAT PROMISE
Genesis Chapters 11, 12

Abraham became the father of faithful people who loved God and fought against Satan. He and his children and their children, and even we who live today (who are faithful), all help to fulfill the promise made to Abraham, wherein God said, "thou shalt be a blessing." One of Abraham's descendants was the greatest blessing of all. His name was Jesus Christ. It was he who would make up for all the bad things that Satan did to Adam and Eve and others.

Abraham was a rich man and had a comfortable home in Ur. Moving must have been a hardship for him and he must have been sad to say goodbye to old friends.

But God had asked Abraham to move, and because he was a prophet he loved God more than his home and all his riches. He packed the things he could take on the backs of his animals and began his long journey. Traveling with Abraham were his wife Sarah, his father Terah, and his nephew Lot. Abraham's servants and their families also went with him. With all the sheep, goats, camels, and cattle, the journey was slow and difficult because most of the land was hot and dry.

THINK ABOUT IT

1. Would you rather have been Abraham or Noah? Why?
2. We know God loved Abraham. Why then do you think Abraham's life seemed hard at times?
3. God made promises to Abraham and he makes them to us. In order to have God's promises fulfilled in our lives what must we do?

NOT THERE YET
Genesis Chapters 11, 12

After moving forward nearly 600 miles the tired travelers arrived at a city named Haran, where some of Abraham's relatives lived. Because Abraham's father was old, the family stayed in Haran several years. Babies were born into the families of the servants. Many of the animals gave birth to young ones. While living in Haran, Abraham told the people there about the true God. Some of them quit worshipping golden statues and worshipped the living God of Abraham. Finally the old father, Terah, died.

It was now time to move on. But Haran seemed like a good home. Why not stay there? Again Abraham heard the voice of God telling him to go on to the Promised Land. As always Abraham obeyed; and so the journey began again. Because the families of the servants were larger in number and some of the faithful people of Haran had decided to go along, the group was even larger than before. Abraham the prophet was indeed blessing the lives of more and more people.

THE PROMISED LAND
Genesis Chapter 12

It can be imagined how one of the children traveling with Abraham might have said to his mother, "I'm tired! When will we get to where we are going?" Abraham might have heard the question and answered, "We'll get there soon and when we do you'll be very happy because we are going to a beautiful land that God promised to give us." Abraham didn't know at that time that many thousands of years later the land to which he was being led would still be called "the Promised Land." Other names by which it is called today are Palestine and Israel.

The tired but happy travelers stopped every night and camped. Each time they did this Abraham built a stone altar and offered a sacrifice as a thanksgiving to God. He told his people that God was with them and that they should always remember him. The people who were already living near Abraham's camp came and listened to him. Some of them worshipped golden gods, but after they had listened to Abraham they decided to forget their golden statues and worship the God of Abraham.

There were no highway signs saying, "Welcome to the Promised Land," but one day the Lord said to Abraham, "Unto thy seed [which meant to him and his family] will I give this land. . . ." Abraham and his small, traveling tent city had arrived in the land that was to be their home forever.

There were people already living in this land who might have wondered, "Will there be a war?" But Abraham loved peace. To avoid trouble he found places where no one else was living and there his people camped. There were streams nearby the places where Abraham and his people pitched their tents of goats' hair. The animals peacefully ate the green grass covering the hillside.

Troy

HITTITE EMPIRE

Kattushash

ARMENIA

Kanish

ASIA MINOR

LYDIA

Sardis

CAPPADOCIA

Tigris R.

Tarsus

Carchemish

AMORITES

LYGIA

Alalakh

Haran

M

Ugarit

Euphrates R.

Alashiya

SYRIA

THE GREAT SEA
(MEDITERRANEAN)

Ma

LEBANON

Mt. Hermon

Tyre

Sidon

Damascus

Sea of Galilee

Nablus

Uru-Salem
Jerusalem

Alexandria

Hebron

Dead Sea

Beersheba

Tanis
(Avaris)

ARABIA

Present
Cairo

WILDERNESS
of
PARAN

Memphis

Ezion-Gebe

EGYPT

Gulf of Suez

Gulf of Aqaba

SINAI

A POOR CHOICE
Genesis Chapters 12-14

Not long after the arriv
of Abraham and his peop

Nile R.

RED
SEA

66

CASPIAN SEA

L. Van

ARARAT MOUNTAINS

ASSYRIA

L. Urmiah

Ecbatana

• Nineveh   • Nuzi

Asshur •

PARTHIA

MEDIA

Present   Present
Baghdad
RAQ

RED LINE INDICATES THE
JOURNEYS OF ABRAHAM

Tigris R.   AKKAD

Babylon •   Susa •

BABYLONIA

Euphrates R.   Ur •

ELAM

CHALDEA

SERT

Persepolis •

PERSIAN
GULF

PERSIA

there came a time when it didn't rain for a long while in the Promised Land. Therefore
there was no food. Abraham was forced to move his people from the Promised Land
southward into Egypt. In this land Abraham was blessed by the Lord and he became
rich. He also was taught many things by God. Abraham and his wife and all of their
people were happy in Egypt; however, there was one big problem—they were in the
wrong place. After some years Abraham "went up out of Egypt, he, and his wife, and
all that he had, and Lot with him. . . ."

Once more, back again in the Promised Land, a most interesting event took place and a very important choice was made. One day Lot said, "Uncle Abraham, the men herding your cattle and the men herding mine have had an argument. My men tell me that your cattle are eating the grass that we had chosen for mine to eat." And Abraham said to Lot, "Let there be no strife, [argument] . . . between me and thee, and between my herdmen and thy herdmen. . . ."

Abraham walked with Lot to the top of a high hill overlooking much land. Abraham thought it would be a good idea if they divided into two groups. He said, "If you go left, I'll go to the right. If you want to go to the right, I'll go to the left."

Lot looked both ways. His heart filled with selfishness as he saw the beautiful Jordan River and the green flatland near to its banks. Nearby were also some cities. He pointed that direction and said, "I'll go down there." Abraham smiled warmly and said, "All right I'll go the other way." It seemed as though Lot was the lucky one because the land left for Abraham was not nearly as good nor as beautiful as that which Lot had chosen.

Lot's selfishness soon brought him sorrow. An army came to fight against the cities nearby to where Lot was camped. The army then also captured Lot and his people and took them away.

Someone ran to Abraham and said, "Lot and his people have been taken prisoners. They need help." Abraham could have said, "Well, it serves him right for being selfish." Instead he, being a kind man, said, "Let us go rescue them."

And that is exactly what they did. They attacked the enemy army and drove it away. They not only rescued Lot and his people, but they also recovered all the things the army had stolen from the people of the nearby cities.

The people were very grateful because Abraham and his men defeated the enemy army and returned their stolen property. Melchizedek, king of the city of Salem, was a priest of the most high God and a very good and faithful man. He, too, was grateful to Abraham and brought him food and gifts. Abraham knew that this man was a high priest of the true God; therefore, he had great respect for Melchizedek. Out of this respect he took one tenth of all his possessions and gave it to Melchizedek. In other words, Abraham paid tithes to Melchizedek, the great high priest.

THINK ABOUT IT

1. Do you think most of the people you know are like Lot or like Abraham? Why?
2. Who are you most like? Why?
3. Why do you suppose Abraham gave one tenth of all he had to the great leader Melchizedek?

A CHILD IS PROMISED
Genesis Chapters 15-18

Abraham did everything that leads to happiness. He tried to keep all of God's commandments. He loved his wife. He was kind to his people and to all those he met. He worshipped God by building altars everywhere he lived. He paid tithes to God's high priest, Melchizedek. He gave other people the best and took what was left. Still, he wasn't quite happy. Do you know why? It was because he didn't have any children. He and his wife were getting very old and it seemed as though he would never have the joy of being a father.

Abraham spent much time studying the stars. One night as he looked at the heavenly bodies, God spoke to him and told him that he would have as many descendants (children, grandchildren, great-grandchildren, and so on) as there were stars! Abraham, who knew the great numbers of stars, was

amazed and asked, "How can that be when I don't even have a child?" God answered him by telling him that he would soon be blessed with a son.

Finally Abraham did have a son, but the mother was one of Abraham's other wives, a woman named Hagar. In those days people often had more than one wife. Yet this son was not the one the Lord had promised Abraham. The promised child would be born of Abraham's first wife, whose name was Sarah.

Abraham loved the child born of Hagar. However, he longed for Sarah to have the promised child, although Sarah was over 90 years old. It should be *impossible* for her to have a child, but nothing is impossible for God if he wants it to happen.

Again God spoke and this time his message was especially for Sarah. He said, ". . . I will bless her, and she shall be *a mother* of nations."

Abraham couldn't believe what God had said. He fell down and laughed. When he told Sarah what God had said, she laughed too; but they laughed too soon.

They learned a lesson that everyone should learn, which is that nothing is too hard for the Lord. Since God is always true to his word, he blessed this wonderful couple with a baby son. Abraham and Sarah smiled as they looked at their newborn child, whom they named Isaac.

THINK ABOUT IT

.. When we think about the birth of Isaac to father Abraham and mother Sarah, what lesson should we learn for our own life?

WICKEDNESS BRINGS DESTRUCTION
Genesis Chapters 18, 19

God and Abraham trusted one another. Therefore, God told Abraham something that was going to happen. Because of the people's great wickedness, the cities of Sodom and Gomorrah were going to be destroyed. Abraham was shocked and saddened when he learned this because it was in those cities that his beloved nephew Lot lived with his family.

Abraham pleaded with the Lord not to destroy the good people in the cities. The Lord was pleased with Abraham's love for people and said, "If I find in Sodom fifty righteous within the city, then I will spare all the place for their sakes."

Abraham was happy, but then he thought, "Maybe there aren't fifty." He asked the Lord, "Would you spare the city if I found forty-five good people?" The Lord agreed. "If there were forty?" Again the Lord agreed. Then Abraham, fearing there weren't even that many, said thirty, then twenty, and finally ten. The Lord agreed that even if there were ten good people he would not destroy the city.

It makes us sad to know that ten good people could have stopped the fire from heaven that destroyed Sodom and Gomorrah. But there were not even ten good people.

Angels warned Lot and his family that the cities would be destroyed. They were told to leave, but most of Lot's family said, "We don't believe you! These cities won't be destroyed." Lot, his wife, and two of their daughters believed the angels and ran for their lives.

They escaped just in time, for behind them they could hear the sounds of the city being destroyed. The angels had told them not to look back.

Tears streamed down their faces as they realized what was happening to their disobedient relatives and friends. Then Lot's wife also disobeyed God. She turned and looked back, and as she did she was turned into a pillar of salt. Lot (finally sitting in a safe place) might have thought, "My selfishness of taking the easy way has brought me and my family much sadness. All of my possessions and most of my family are gone." He must have shed great tears of sorrow on that sad day.

THINK ABOUT IT

1. If God had sent you to the cities of Sodom and Gomorrah, what would you have told the people to try to get them to change so that they wouldn't be destroyed?

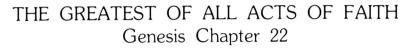

THE GREATEST OF ALL ACTS OF FAITH
Genesis Chapter 22

Abraham (now over 100 years old) had done many difficult things in his life. Even now as he prayed to the Lord his greatest test was about to begin. He could hardly believe what the Lord was saying. It couldn't be. God was asking him to take his young son Isaac, place him on an altar, and offer him as a sacrifice.

That night Abraham could not sleep. He had waited so long for his dear son Isaac to be born. He loved this young man more than he loved himself. No one could have been more sad than this good prophet, who might soon see his own son die.

But Abraham always obeyed and trusted God. The next day the son, the father, a small donkey, and two servants walked out into the wilderness. For three days the sad journey went on toward a high mountain. As they walked along, Abraham must have wondered over and over again, "How can God's promises be fulfilled if my son is dead? How then will I have children and grandchildren?"

Finally the mountain where the sacrifice
was to take place was in sight. Abraham told
his servants to wait, and he and his son
continued on alone. Isaac, who knew nothing
of what was to happen, wondered why there
was no animal to sacrifice. He asked, "Behold
the fire and the wood: but where *is* the lamb
for a burnt offering?" Abraham sadly replied,
"My son, God will provide himself a lamb. . . ."

At the place where the sacrifice was to be offered, young Isaac's mind and heart were filled with wonder. "Where was the lamb?" With tears in his eyes he probably saw the look of sadness on his father's face. Perhaps somehow he knew now that he was to be the lamb. He could have run away, for he was young and his father was old, but Isaac didn't make any attempt to escape for he trusted his father with all his heart and he knew that whatever was to be done would be the will of God.

Isaac was bound by ropes and placed upon the altar. There was no one there to witness this tender, heartbroken father's tears. As the Lord considered the faith and trust of his great prophet Abraham, perhaps he joined his tears with this mighty man. God also knew that what he had asked of Abraham, he himself would one day do. For in the future his Son, Jesus Christ, would also be used as a lamb for a sacrifice.

Without doubt this was one of the greatest religious moments in history. Would Abraham's faith falter? Could he do it? Abraham stretched forth his hand, and took the knife to slay his son.

Just as Isaac was about to die at the hand of his own father, the Lord spoke, "Lay not thine hand upon the lad, . . . for now I know that thou fearest God, seeing thou hast not withheld thy son, thine only *son* from me."

Imagine the joy of Abraham as with trembling hands he quickly untied his son. The two of them fell into each others arms. The greatest test ever given to man was over, and the man who had passed the test was the same one who had been given God's greatest promise. That man was the prophet Abraham.

A lamb caught in a thicket nearby was sacrificed. Someday God would experience great sorrow himself when his own Son would not be spared as Isaac had been. His Son would die. At that time when Jesus would die on the cross, Satan's plan, which began in the Garden of Eden, would begin to be destroyed.

THINK ABOUT IT

1. If someone asked you to tell him what you considered to be the greatest act of faith you've ever heard about, what would it be?
2. Has God ever asked you to do something that is really difficult that would take a great deal of faith? What was it?
3. How was that which God asked Abraham to do exactly like what he, our Heavenly Father, would someday do?

CHOOSING JUST THE RIGHT WIFE
Genesis Chapters 23, 24

Having passed God's great test together caused Abraham and his son Isaac to be even closer. They often talked of life and death and of eternity. Life is so good when Children and parents love each other and feel happy to be together. Abraham, Sarah, and Isaac talked about whom Isaac would marry. They didn't want him to marry a girl who was not of his faith and who didn't believe in the true God.

A few years later a great sadness came to Abraham and Isaac. Sarah, the beloved wife and mother, died and was buried. With Sarah gone Isaac longed even more to be married. he was now forty years old. Isaac was thrilled as he heard his father, Abraham, say, "My son, I'm going to send my trusted servant up to Haran to find you a wife." That's the way marriages were arranged in those days. Isaac probably wished he could go himself but if that couldn't be, then he probably said to the servant, "Be sure to find me a very good woman, and it would be nice if she were pretty, too."

The servant went on his journey. After a long trip he and the caravan arrived in Haran. All the travelers and their animals were tired and thirsty, so they went to the city well to get water.

In those days the young girls came to the well to get water for the family. Abraham's servant prayed that he would be led to just the right

young lady. Finding the perfect one for someone else was a most difficult task. The servant's mind was filled with worry as girls came one by one to the well. Whenever a pretty one came, he wondered, "How can I know that she is not selfish and proud."

The servant then prayed again. This time he said, "When I see the one I feel is the right one, I'll ask her to give me a drink. If she says, 'I will, and I'll also give water to your camels,' then I'll know she is the one." The prayer was answered.

Soon beautiful Rebekah arrived at the well. In response to the servant's request she gave him water. Then she also gave water to the camels. She was both good and beautiful!

Arrangements were made with her father for Rebekah to marry Isaac. Saying goodbye to her family was sad for Rebekah, but she looked forward to her new life. She traveled with the servant to the Promised Land. When she saw Isaac she was thrilled. "And Isaac brought her into his mother Sarah's tent, and took Rebekah, and she became his wife; and he loved her. . . ."

THINK ABOUT IT

1. Why is it so important that we choose the right friends?
2. After saying your prayers have you ever been guided like the servant who picked out the wife for Isaac? What happened?
3. What can we tell about Rebekah by the fact that she not only was willing to give water to the servant but also to his animals?

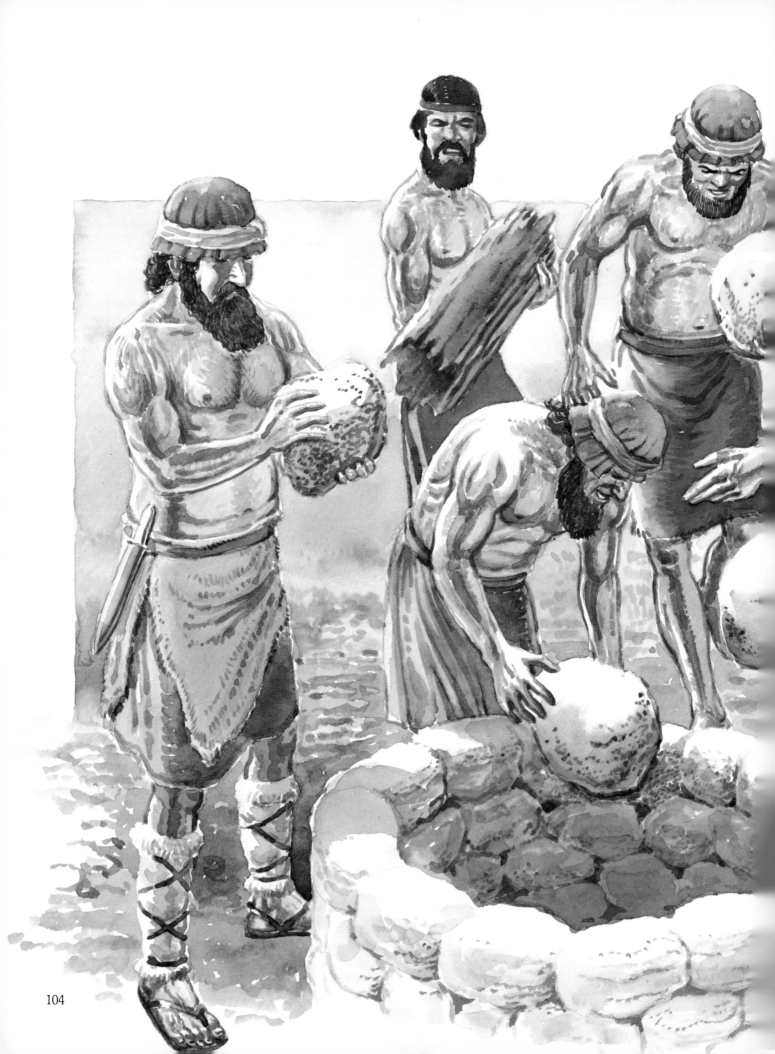

THE MAN WHO LOVED PEACE
Genesis Chapter 26

What would a farmer do if he had dug wells to get water for his animals and then his neighbors came and threw rocks and dirt in the wells so that he couldn't get the water out?

That's what happened to Abraham's kind and generous son, Isaac. The Philistines, who lived in the same country, were jealous that Isaac's herds were better than theirs, so they filled up his wells with dirt. What Isaac did is rather surprising. He didn't fight back, even though he had many men and probably could have won a fight with his cruel neighbors. He chose to have peace rather than fight. He told his people, "Let's move on. We can dig some more wells."

But after digging more wells, the Philistines repeated their evil deeds. Isaac's men probably said, "The Philistines have done it again. Let's go beat them up." Again Isaac's answer was, "We don't want trouble. We can move again and dig more wells."

By this time the Philistines began to wonder about Isaac. This great man was different than other men. They began to fear that he might come and destroy them, so they came to him and begged him not to do so. When he told them he wouldn't ever do that because he wanted to be their friend, they decided never to bother him again. Because Isaac was so kind and unselfish, ". . . the Lord blessed him . . . and [he] grew until he became very great."

Isaac's father, Abraham, lived a life of many adventures, as did Isaac's son, Jacob. But Isaac himself didn't have nearly as many exciting things happen to him. When all three of these men had died, it is interesting to know who the people decided deserved the greatest monument. It was the man who loved peace more than fighting—the man who was so unselfish—it was the great man Isaac.

THINK ABOUT IT

1. Do you think Isaac was strong or weak when he refused to go to battle against those who were filling up his wells with dirt? Why?

108

GIVING UP EVERYTHING FOR A BOWL OF SOUP
Genesis Chapter 25

"Twins! It's twins!", shouted the servant of Isaac and Rebekah. Yes, it was twins. The great love of this man of peace and his bride (chosen because she was so kind at the well) was now blessed, not with one baby, but with two: Esau and Jacob!

In those days the first son born into a family was given something called the birthright. The birthright meant that this son had the right to almost all of his father's possessions. He also had the right to receive a special blessing appointing him to be the family leader after the father's death.

Even though these two little babies were twins, Esau was the first born and Jacob, who arrived into the world just a few seconds later, was the second. Thus Esau should have been the one to receive the birthright, but it didn't turn out that way. It is interesting to read how the birthright finally was given to Jacob rather than Esau.

Esau was a handsome, fun-loving boy. He liked to hunt and do other adventurous things. His father, Isaac, loved him but worried about him. Esau had much to do to get ready to be the family leader, but he didn't seem to care about that. All he wanted to do was to have a good time. Jacob was more serious and Rebekah felt that Jacob would make a better leader.

Jacob also wondered about the future. He knew that his grandfather Abraham had been told by the Lord that his family would be a blessing to all other families who would ever live upon the earth. This same blessing was given to his father, Isaac. How could such an important blessing be given to his carefree brother?

One day Esau came home from hunting tired and hungry. Jacob had just finished cooking some soup (pottage) that smelled delicious. Esau shouted with glee, "Give me some of that food." Jacob replied, "I will if you will sell me your birthright today."

"And Esau said, Behold, I *am* at the point to die: and what profit shall this birthright do to me?" And so it was that Esau willingly gave up everything that was really important for just a few minutes pleasure in eating.

THINK ABOUT IT

1. If you are going to be a leader in life, whom do you want to pattern your life after—Esau or Jacob? Why?
2. Have you ever known anyone who gave up almost everything for some selfish reason? What did they do?
3. What can we learn from the story of the lost birthright?

JACOB RECEIVES THE PROMISE
Genesis Chapter 27

Years went by. Esau knew that he no longer had the birthright, as Jacob and their mother, Rebekah, also knew. But his father, Isaac, didn't know. By now Isaac was very old and he knew he would soon die. He called his son Esau to him and told him that it was time for him to give Esau the great blessing of God and make him the family leader. Before he was to receive the blessing, Isaac said to his son Esau, "Take your bow and arrow and go out and kill a deer, and make me some of the savory meat that I like so much; and when you've done that I will bless you."

Esau departed, and while he was gone Rebekah did a most amazing thing. She overheard what Isaac had told Esau, so she told Jacob to quickly kill a lamb. She would cook it and Jacob could take it to his father. Jacob knew that Isaac was nearly blind and wouldn't be able to recognize him from Esau. But he worried and said, "Behold Esau my brother *is* a hairy man, and I *am* a smooth man:

My father . . . will feel me, and I shall seem to him as a deceiver; and I shall bring a curse upon me, and not a blessing."

Rebekah, who felt that Jacob should receive the blessing, told him not to worry. She said that if anything went wrong she would take the blame. Rebekah got some of Esau's clothes and told Jacob to put them on. She also tied some furry skin to Jacob's hands. Soon all was ready.

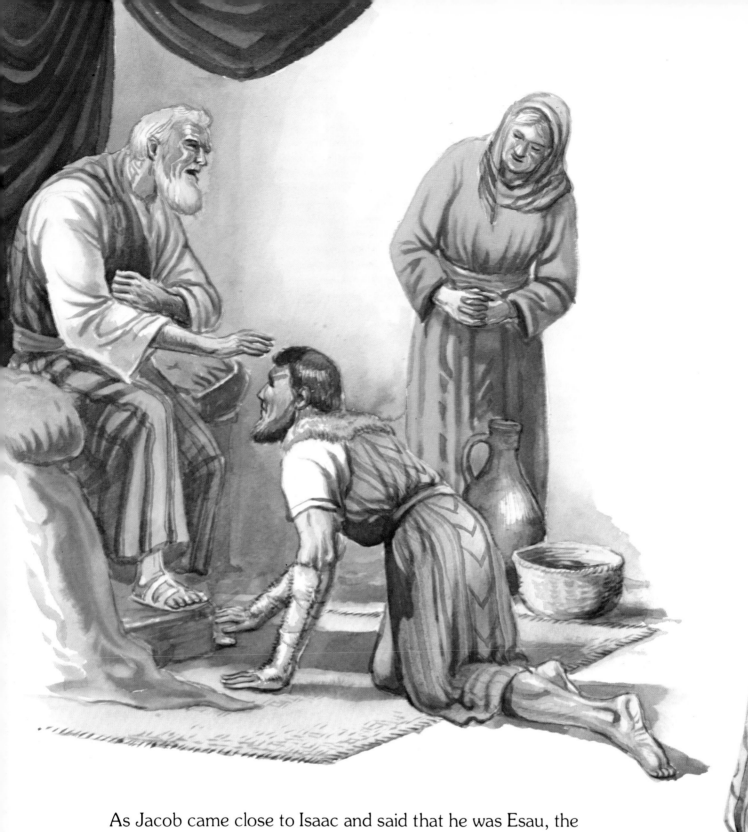

As Jacob came close to Isaac and said that he was Esau, the old father thought it sounded like Jacob. He asked to touch his son's hands. As he did so, Jacob's heart pounded with fear. Slowly the old man's hand rubbed across the hairy fur. Isaac then smiled, for he was satisfied that it was Esau since he knew that Jacob did not have such hairy hands.

The great blessing that Isaac thought he was giving to Esau was given to Jacob. But God, who was really giving the blessing, knew who was receiving it and he wanted Jacob to be the new leader because he was more faithful. Thus, like his grandfather Abraham and his father, Isaac, Jacob was given the blessing that through him and his family all the families of the earth would be blessed.

When Esau returned and learned what had happened he became very angry. Suddenly he decided he wanted the birthright and the blessings, but it was too late. Esau cried unto his father to bless him also. Esau's blessing was that he would live by the sword and serve his brother. This made him even more angry and he decided he would get even. He would kill his brother. How different it would have been if Esau had kept the commandments of the Lord and had been worthy. There is so much sorrow in the world because some children cannot be trusted. They give up every good thing just because they want to do everything their own selfish way. They give up lasting happiness and peace out of anger or for a brief moment of excitement.

THINK ABOUT IT

1. Do you think Esau should have been angry when he realized that Jacob had received the great blessing? Why?

FEAR TURNS TO HAPPINESS
Genesis Chapters 27, 28

"Run for your life," Rebekah told her son Jacob. "Go to Haran, my old home town." Jacob sadly packed a few possessions and departed. His heart was confused and frightened.

When a person is homesick the dark nights are often the saddest times. Jacob was alone in the mountains. He had a hard time falling asleep, but when he did he began to dream.

In his dream he saw a ladder. Angels were going up and down on the ladder, and at the top was heaven. In the dream the Lord told Jacob, "I *am* the Lord God of Abraham thy father, and the God of Isaac: the land whereon thou liest, to thee will I give it, and to thy seed [family]. . . ." He also told Jacob that his family would be large and would be a blessing to all other families.

When Jacob woke up he was no longer sad and discouraged or afraid. He knew God was with him. Many people are like Jacob. When they are afraid all they need to know is that God is near. When they know that they are no longer frightened. Jacob had worried about what he and Rebekah had done to Esau. He wondered if God would forgive him. Now he knew that God did forgive him and that there was a ladder to climb. If he climbed it with the angels he could reach heaven. Jacob was very happy as he built an altar to his God and then hurried on toward Haran.

THINK ABOUT IT

1. Have you ever been sad and discouraged or perhaps homesick as Jacob was? What was it like?
2. How could prayer help you as it did Jacob?

PATIENCE BRINGS HAPPINESS
Genesis Chapter 29

"There it is," said Jacob as he looked ahead and saw Haran. He was tired and thirsty and headed right to a well just outside the city. Then for a moment he forgot his tiredness and thirst, for there at the well with her sheep was the most beautiful girl he had ever seen.

She was just about to move a stone off the top of the well. Jacob said, "Here, let me do that." He also helped her water her sheep. As they talked, Jacob told her who he was. She told him that her name was Rachel, and they learned that they were related. In those days it was all right to marry a relative and perhaps they were already beginning to think that marriage would be a good idea.

Rachel's father, named Laban, was pleased when a few days later Jacob said, "I want to marry your daughter." Laban agreed but said, "If you want her you must work for me for seven years." Jacob couldn't go home and he needed work, so he gladly agreed.

But Laban was not an honest man. He tricked Jacob. After seven years Jacob was not given Rachel but instead her sister, whose name was Leah.

Laban probably smiled as Jacob shouted that it was not fair. "I was promised Rachel." Laban replied, "It must not be so done in our country, to give the younger before the firstborn." Then Laban offered to give Rachel also if Jacob would work for another seven years. Jacob argued, but it was no use. He finally decided that Rachel was worth another seven years' work. Thus Laban "gave him Rachel his daughter to wife also . . . and [Jacob] served with him yet seven other years."

As in Jacob's case, some things are worth waiting and working for. Sometimes a person wants to grow up too soon, to go away from home too soon, to quit school too soon, or to get married too soon. But by waiting and working (like Jacob and Rachel) he will someday be blessed and very happy.

THINK ABOUT IT

1. Jacob had a goal to marry Rachel but he had to work and wait in order to do that. What are some of the things that you want to have in life and how are you preparing and working so that you can someday have them?

Eve
B. 0

Adam
B. 0
D. 930

Seth
B. 130
D. 1042

Enos
B. 235
D. 1140

Cainan
B. 325
D. 1235

Mahalaleel
B. 395
D. 1290

Terah
B. 1878
D. 2083

Nahor
B. 1849
D. 1997

S
B.
D.

Abram (Abraham)
B. 1948
D. 2123

NOTE: Birth and death dates are only approximate and are
counted in years after the beginning of Adam's life.